Barbec

CAROLE HANDSLIP

MEREHURST

LONDON

Contents

Introduction 3

Barbecued Fish 4

Barbecued Meat 14

Barbecued Vegetables 40

Salads & Accompaniments 46

Patio Meals 56

Desserts & Drinks 70

Index 80

Managing Editor: Janet Illsley
Photographer: Alan Newnham
Designer: Sue Storey
Food Stylist: Carole Handslip
Photographic Stylist: Maria Jacques
Typeset by Angel Graphics
Colour separation by Fotographics, UK - Hong Kong
Printed in Italy by New Interlitho S.p.A.

Published 1991 by Merehurst Ltd,
Ferry House, 51/57 Lacy Road, Putney, London SW15 1PR

© Merehurst Ltd

ISBN: 1 85391 141 0 (Cased)
ISBN: 1 85391 245 X (Paperback)

NOTES
All spoon measures are level: 1 tablespoon = 15ml spoon;
1 teaspoon = 5ml spoon. Use fresh herbs and freshly ground black
pepper unless otherwise stated.

Introduction

Barbecues are ideal for relaxed, informal entertaining in summer. They are easy, appetizing and fun – and they have the added advantage that others usually join in the cooking! Organisation is the key to a successful barbecue. Check that you have everything at hand to avoid endless trips back to the house – including long-handled tongs, a fish slice, oven gloves, oil and basting brush, kitchen paper and a water spray to douse flames. Have serving plates, cutlery and accompaniments ready too.

To prepare the barbecue, arrange the charcoal in a pyramid, intersperse with solid fuel tablets and set alight. Make sure you allow enough time for the coals to heat up before cooking. Charcoal chips usually takes 45-60 minutes; briquettes, a little less. Test by holding your hand at grid level: if you can stand the heat for *no more than* 2-3 seconds, the coals are ready. Oil the grid and level the coals with tongs before cooking.

Serving a variety of different foods makes a barbecue more interesting, but you will need to cook them in a logical order. Obviously items which take longest to cook must be added to the barbecue first. Cooking times vary enormously – depending on the heat of the coals, wind strength, etc – so use my suggested times as a guide only. You can adjust the heat as necessary by raising or lowering the grid, or by moving food towards, or away from, the hottest area.

On a hot sunny day or a balmy summer evening nothing surpasses the aroma of food cooking over a charcoal fire. But for *al fresco* occasions when you prefer to have everything prepared and cooked ahead I have included a selection of cold patio meals too. I hope my ideas will tempt you to eat in the garden as soon as the weather permits.

Carole Handship.

Barbecued Prawns

In my view there is no better way to eat prawns, and the aroma is wonderful. You could use cooked king prawns, but barbecue them very briefly or they will become tough. A delightful nibble whilst waiting for the main course.

16 raw king prawns, heads and tails removed
¼ teaspoon paprika
¼ teaspoon pepper
¼ teaspoon salt
pinch of chilli powder
olive oil for brushing

1 Make a cut along the underside of each prawn, taking care not to cut right through the shell. Open out, flatten and remove the black intestinal thread.
2 Mix the seasoning ingredients together and sprinkle over the prawns. Brush with oil, place on a hinged grid and barbecue the shell side for 3-4 minutes. Turn and cook for 1-2 minutes. Serve immediately. *Serves 4-6.*

Spanish Sardines

1kg (2lb) fresh sardines
4 tablespoons olive oil
juice of 1 lemon
2 tablespoons chopped parsley
salt and pepper to taste
lemon wedges to serve

1 Scale the sardines by gently scraping from tail to head with the back of a small knife. Using scissors, cut off the fins, then make a slit in the underside and remove the intestines. Wash thoroughly, then dry with kitchen paper.
2 Mix the oil, lemon juice, parsley and seasoning together in a shallow dish. Add the sardines and turn to coat completely. Put into a metal fish grid, or thread through the heads on to skewers.
3 Barbecue for 3-5 minutes each side until crisp, brushing with marinade occasionally. Serve with any remaining marinade poured over, and accompany with lemon wedges and French bread. *Serves 4.*

Scallop & Bacon Kebabs

Bacon-wrapped scallops are delicious cooked on the barbecue. The delicate scallop flesh is protected, remaining succulent inside the crisp bacon. Being fairly quick to cook they make an ideal starter to serve while waiting for other barbecued foods. If serving as a main course, accompany with rice and a green salad.

12 scallops, halved
12 rashers streaky bacon, rinds
  removed
MARINADE:
1 clove garlic, finely chopped
1 tablespoon chopped fennel
2 tablespoons olive oil
1 tablespoon lemon juice

FENNEL MAYONNAISE:
60ml (2 fl oz/¹/₄ cup)
  mayonnaise
60ml (2 fl oz/¹/₄ cup) natural
  yogurt
1 tablespoon chopped fennel
1 tablespoon Pernod (optional)
salt and pepper to taste

1 To make the marinade, mix the garlic, fennel, oil and lemon juice together in a bowl. Add the scallops to the marinade, mix well and leave for 30 minutes.
2 Stretch the bacon with the back of a knife until thin, then cut each rasher in half.
3 Lift the scallops from the marinade and wrap each one in a piece of bacon. Thread on to 4 long skewers.
4 To make the mayonnaise, mix all the ingredients together in a bowl.
5 Barbecue the kebabs for 8-10 minutes, turning occasionally. Serve immediately, with the fennel mayonnaise. *Serves 4.*

SALMON BROCHETTES: In place of the bacon-wrapped scallops, use 375g (12oz) each salmon and monkfish (or kingfish). Cut into 2.5cm (1 inch) squares and marinate (as above) in the refrigerator for 2 hours. Thread on to wooden skewers and cook as above. Serve as a main course.

Illustrated opposite: Salmon brochettes (above); Scallop & bacon kebabs (below).

Spiced Fish Kebabs

Any firm fleshed fish can be used for these kebabs: try tuna, monk-fish (or kingfish) if you prefer. Unlike whole fish, steaks and cubed fish are improved by marinating. Yellow fried rice makes a good accompaniment.

500g (1lb) swordfish or halibut
MARINADE:
1 teaspoon tandoori spice mix
155ml (5 fl oz/²/₃ cup) natural
  yogurt
2 tablespoons sunflower oil

juice of ¹/₂ lemon
15g (¹/₂oz) creamed coconut,
  blended with 1 tablespoon
  boiling water
TO SERVE:
lemon wedges

1 Cut the fish into 2.5cm (1 inch) cubes and put into a shallow dish.
2 Mix all the marinade ingredients together in a bowl until smooth, then pour over the fish. Turn to coat completely and leave to marinate for 2 hours.
3 Lift the fish out of the marinade, thread on to skewers and barbecue for 8-10 minutes, brushing with extra marinade and turning occasionally. Serve with lemon wedges and yellow fried rice (page 24.) *Serves 4.*

HERBY FISH KEBABS: As an alternative, use a herb marinade. Mix together 3 tablespoons olive oil, 3 tablespoons lemon juice and 1 tablespoon chopped herbs, such as parsley, thyme, dill or fennel. Season to taste. Marinate fish for 2 hours, then thread onto skewers interspersing with bay leaves. Cook as above.

BARBECUED FISH STEAKS: Buy thick steaks, or they will dry out over the barbecue. Cover with the marinade, leave for 2 hours, then cook for 10-15 minutes, turning once.

Illustrated opposite: Herby fish kebabs (above); Spiced fish kebabs (below).

Barbecued Fish with Fennel

There are several varieties of whole fish which are particularly suited to cooking over a charcoal fire. Grey mullet, red mullet, trout, bream, salmon, grouper and mackerel are all good, but sea bass is, I think, the nicest of all. It needs no adornment – save for a few lemon wedges – but I sometimes serve it with fennel mayonnaise and a cucumber salad.

Whole fish do not really benefit from a marinade, but adding herbs – such as fennel, bay, thyme or rosemary – to the fire toward the end of cooking, imparts a wonderful aroma and flavour to the fish. Moistening these herbs first with water gives a more pronounced smokey flavour.

You can cook whole fish with the scales intact – they provide protection from the fire – but as I prefer to eat the crispened skin, I always scale the fish first.

1 sea bass (or grouper),
 weighing about 1kg (2lb),
 gutted
salt and pepper to taste
few fennel sprigs
olive oil for brushing

TO SERVE:
lemon wedges and fennel sprigs
fennel mayonnaise (page 7),
 (optional)

1 Scale the fish by scraping from tail to head with the back of a small knife, or ask your fishmonger to do so. Make 3 deep diagonal slashes on each side of the fish to allow the heat to penetrate.

2 Season the inside of the fish and insert fennel sprigs. Brush the outside liberally with oil and season.

3 Lay the fish in a hinged grid and barbecue for 10-15 minutes on each side, brushing with more oil occasionally.

4 Divide into portions and garnish with lemon wedges and fennel. Serve with fennel mayonnaise, crusty bread and a leafy salad or cucumber salad (below). *Serves 4.*

CUCUMBER SALAD: Mix together 3 tablespoons white wine vinegar, 1 tablespoon clear honey and 2 tablespoons chopped dill or fennel. Pour over 1 peeled and sliced cucumber.

Marinated Halibut Steaks

A simple marinade, but a superb combination of flavours to complement fish. Other fish steaks, such as shark or tuna, would also be suitable. I like to serve this dish with garlic bread and a crisp green salad.

2 or 4 halibut steaks
MARINADE:
2 cloves garlic, crushed
1 teaspoon finely chopped fresh
    root (green) ginger

1 tablespoon sesame oil
1 tablespoon soy sauce
3 tablespoons dry sherry
2 spring onions (green shallots),
    sliced diagonally

1 Mix all the marinade ingredients together in a bowl.
2 Lay the halibut steaks in a shallow dish and pour over the marinade. Cover and leave to marinate in the refrigerator for 2 hours.
3 Lift the fish steaks out of the marinade and barbecue for 4-6 minutes on each side, depending on the thickness. Serve immediately. *Serves 2 or 4.*

GARLIC BREAD: Cream 90g (3oz) butter with 2 crushed garlic cloves and seasoning to taste. Slice a French stick diagonally, without cutting right through so the loaf holds together. Spread both sides of the slices with garlic butter. Wrap in foil and barbecue for 15 minutes. Unwrap and crispen for 2-3 minutes.

FLOWER POT BARBECUE: When there are only two of you try this wonderful Portuguese idea. Half-fill a 25cm (10 inch) clay flower pot with gravel and cover with charcoal chips to within 2.5cm (1 inch) of the top. Lay a grid on the flower pot or balance skewers across the rim to cook the food. You can conveniently position this barbecue next to the table. Clean after use to prevent the ash clogging the air flow through the gravel.

Yogurtlu Kebab

A really tasty Turkish dish of barbecued lamb, served on crisp slices of pitta, topped with tomato sauce, creamy yogurt and chopped parsley. Remember to take a sharp knife and a board to the barbecue for slicing the pitta.

750g (1½lb) boned leg of lamb,
  cut into large cubes
salt and pepper to taste
2 red peppers, seeded and cut
  into large squares
4 pitta breads
155ml (5 fl oz/⅔ cup) Greek
  yogurt
4 tablespoons chopped parsley

MARINADE:
4 tablespoons olive oil
2 cloves garlic, crushed
juice of ½ lemon
TOMATO SAUCE:
2 tablespoons olive oil
1 clove garlic, crushed
500g (1lb) tomatoes, skinned
  and chopped

1 Mix the marinade ingredients together in a shallow dish, add the seasoned lamb chunks and turn until evenly coated. Leave to marinate for 2 hours.

2 To make the tomato sauce, heat the oil in a pan, add the garlic and fry for 1 minute, then add the tomatoes with seasoning. Cook for 5 minutes; set aside.

3 Remove meat from marinade and thread on to skewers, alternately with red pepper squares. Take to the barbecue with the hot tomato sauce, pitta bread, yogurt and parsley.

4 Brush kebabs with marinade and barbecue for 10-12 minutes, turning and brushing with marinade as they cook.

5 Put the pan of tomato sauce on the barbecue to keep warm. Heat the pitta breads on the barbecue until crisp.

6 Slice the pitta and place on the serving dish. Remove lamb from skewers and put on the pitta. Pour over the tomato sauce, swirl on the yogurt and top with parsley. *Serves 4.*

SIS KEBAB: Marinate the lamb as above, then thread onto skewers interspersing with red and green pepper squares, and onion wedges. Barbecue as above, then serve with pitta bread and tomato, cucumber and onion salad (page 50).

Adana Kebab

I first tasted this delicious, spicy kebab in a little town on the south coast of Turkey. If your preference is for really spicy hot flavours, add more chillies! I like to make mini-sized kebabs (see below), either to serve as an appetizer while waiting for the large ones to cook, or as a nibble at a summer drinks party.

60g (2oz) bread, crusts removed
750g (1½lb) lean minced lamb
1 egg
3 cloves garlic, crushed
3 green chillies, seeded and
  finely chopped
1 onion, finely chopped

2 teaspoons ground cumin
2 teaspoons paprika
1 teaspoon tabasco sauce
1 tablespoon chopped parsley
1 teaspoon salt
½ teaspoon pepper

1 Put the bread in a small bowl, pour over water to cover and soak for a few minutes, then squeeze dry. Place bread in a mixing bowl or food processor and add all the remaining ingredients. Process or work together by hand until smooth; it is essential to mix thoroughly to ensure the mixture binds together well and moulds easily.

2 Divide mixture into 16 pieces, each about the size of an egg. Using dampened hands, shape into long, thin sausages. Insert a skewer into each one and mould to a good shape.

3 Brush the kebabs liberally with oil and barbecue for 10-15 minutes, turning to ensure they cook evenly. Serve with pitta bread, tomato and onion salad and caçik (below). *Makes 16.*

MINI KEBABS: Take small pieces of the mixture, about the size of a cherry, and mould each on to one end of a satay stick. Oil generously and barbecue for 5 minutes, turning several times.

CAÇIK: Peel and grate ½ cucumber, drain and mix into 250ml (8 fl oz/1 cup) strained Greek yogurt with 1 crushed garlic clove, 1 tablespoon chopped dill and seasoning.

Spit Roast Lamb

Spit roasting a whole lamb is usually impracticable, but a leg of lamb is manageable, even on a small barbecue.

An inexpensive battery operated spit is useful for chicken and joints of meat. When spit roasting any large joint, you need all round heat, so push the barbecue coals away from the centre to form a hollow. Put a foil tray in the centre space to catch the juices; this also prevents flare-ups.

The cooking time will vary, depending on how you like your lamb cooked – I prefer to eat it slightly pink, accompanied by gratin dauphinois, creamy barbecued garlic and a crisp salad.

1 leg of lamb, weighing about
   2-2.25kg (4-4½lb)
3 cloves garlic, sliced

small bunch of rosemary sprigs
olive oil for basting
salt and pepper to taste

1 Make deep incisions in the lamb at regular intervals, then insert slices of garlic and small sprigs of rosemary. Rub all over with olive oil and seasoning.

2 Fix the joint on the spit, making sure it is evenly balanced and cook over the barbecue for 1-1¼ hours, turning (if necessary) and basting occasionally with olive oil. Lay sprigs of rosemary on the coals toward the end of cooking, for extra aroma and flavour; you can also use a rosemary brush (see page 41) for basting.

3 Test the meat with a skewer to see if it is cooked: if the juices are very pink, the meat will be undercooked; if slightly pink the lamb is ready.

4 Take the lamb off the spit, put onto a board, cover with foil, and leave to rest for 10 minutes; this will make it easier to carve. Serve with a salad or barbecued vegetables (page 42) and gratin dauphinois (page 54). *Serves 6.*

SPIT ROAST CHICKEN WITH TARRAGON: Use a chicken, weighing about 2kg (4lb). Insert sprigs of tarragon into the cavity, season and baste with olive oil. Barbecue for 1-1½ hours until the skin is crisp and the juices run clear when the thighs are pieced with a skewer.

Homemade Burgers

A hinged wire holder is most useful for cooking burgers and fish which are inclined to break up as you turn them. Either serve these burgers the traditional way in a bun with relishes, or with spiced bean salad (page 52) and crisp salad leaves.

BURGERS:
60g (2oz/1 cup) wholemeal
   breadcrumbs
2 tablespoons water
500g (1lb) best quality lean
   minced beef
1 onion, finely chopped
1 clove garlic, crushed
1 tablespoon soy sauce
2 tablespoons chopped parsley
1 tablespoon chopped thyme
salt and pepper to taste
oil for brushing

MIXED PEPPER RELISH:
3 tablespoons olive oil
1 onion, chopped
2 red peppers, seeded and
   chopped
1 green pepper, seeded and
   chopped
3 cloves garlic, crushed
$1/4$ teaspoon chilli powder
2 tablespoons clear honey
90ml (3 fl oz/$1/3$ cup) wine
   vinegar
90ml (3 fl oz/$1/3$ cup) tomato
   juice

1 To make the burgers, put the breadcrumbs into a bowl, sprinkle with the water and leave for 5 minutes. Add the beef, together with all the remaining ingredients. Work thoroughly using your hands, until evenly mixed.

2 Divide the mixture into 4 portions and, using dampened hands, shape into balls. Flatten to 10cm (4 inch) rounds, about 1.5cm (¾ inch) thick. Chill until required.

3 To make the relish, heat the oil in a pan, add the onion and peppers and fry for 10 minutes, stirring occasionally. Add the garlic, chilli powder, honey, vinegar and tomato juice; simmer for 5-10 minutes until soft and pulpy.

4 Barbecue the burgers for 5-8 minutes on each side according to taste, basting frequently with oil. Serve in buns if desired, with the pepper relish. *Serves 4.*

VENISON BURGERS: Replace the beef with ground venison, and add 2 tablespoons tomato purée (paste) to the mixture.

Mexican Marinated Beef

This recipe features a fairly hot, spicy marinade, but you can always omit a chilli if you prefer. I like to serve this with spiced beans (page 52) to complete a typically Mexican barbecue.

750g (1½lb) rump steak
125g (4.4oz) packet tostada
  shells (fried corn pancakes)
MARINADE:
3 tablespoons oil (see note)
3 tablespoons red wine
1 tablespoon chopped coriander
  leaves
2 green chillies, seeded and
  finely chopped
salt and pepper to taste

GUACAMOLE:
1 large avocado
juice of ½ lemon
2 spring onions (green shallots),
  chopped
3 tomatoes, skinned and
  chopped
1 tablespoon chopped coriander
  leaves
¼ teaspoon chilli powder
1 teaspoon salt

1 To make the marinade, mix all the ingredients together in a small bowl. Put the steak into a shallow dish, pour over the marinade and leave for about 2 hours.

2 Meanwhile make the guacamole. Halve, stone and peel the avocado, then mash with the lemon juice, using a fork. Transfer to a bowl, add the remaining ingredients and stir well.

3 Lift the steak out of the marinade and barbecue for about 6 minutes on each side, brushing occasionally with the marinade. Put the tortillas on the barbecue to crispen.

4 Slice the steak thinly on a board and place on a warmed serving dish. Serve with the tortillas and guacamole. Serves 4.

NOTE: Flavoured oils are useful for barbecue marinades. You can use dried chillies, garlic, root ginger or herbs, such as rosemary or thyme. Flavour sunflower oil with spices; olive oil with herbs. Add the flavouring to the oil and leave for about 4 weeks before using.

Beef Teryaki

A Japanese 'glaze-grilled' dish: *teri* meaning shiny; *yaki*, grilled. Many foods may be cooked in the teryaki style – fish, steak, chicken and pork are all suitable. I like to marinade the meat for about 4 hours, but even after 1 hour it has acquired quite a good flavour. You may find it easier to crush the ginger in a garlic press – peel and roughly chop it first.

You will need about 16 satay sticks; soak these in cold water before use and they will be less likely to burn.

500g (1lb) rump steak, 2cm
(3/4 inch) thick
MARINADE:
3 tablespoons soy sauce
2 tablespoons sherry or saké

2 cloves garlic crushed
2.5cm (1 inch) piece fresh root
(green) ginger, peeled and
crushed
1 tablespoon sesame oil

1 Cut the beef into strips, about 5mm (1/4 inch) wide by 13cm (5 inches) long.
2 Mix all the marinade ingredients together in a shallow dish. Add the steak, turn to coat evenly and leave to marinate for about 4 hours in the refrigerator.
3 Weave the strips on to wooden satay sticks, to resemble snakes. Barbecue for about 4-5 minutes until tender, turning once. Serve with yellow fried rice (below) and oriental salad (page 50). *Serves 4-8.*

YELLOW FRIED RICE: Heat 2 tablespoons sunflower oil in a frying pan and fry 1 chopped onion until pale golden. Add 1/2 teaspoon turmeric and fry for 1 minute. Add 500g (1lb/3 cups) cooked rice and cook, stirring, until evenly coloured and heated through.

Fillet Steak on Garlic Toast

The best toast is made on a charcoal fire – it's even better spread with garlic butter, and makes a perfect bed for serving rump steak and other meats, such as liver and kidney.

In the Spanish region of Catalonia 'Pan amb oli' is a speciality. It is a thick slice of charcoal toasted bread, spread with garlic, olive oil and tomato pulp – delicious! The Italian, 'bruschetta' is similar.

4 fillet steaks, each about
185g (6oz)
MARINADE:
3 tablespoons red wine
3 tablespoons olive oil
2 cloves garlic, chopped
few thyme sprigs
salt and pepper to taste

GARLIC TOAST:
60g (2oz) butter
2 cloves garlic
4 thick slices bread
HORSERADISH RELISH:
2 tablespoons natural yogurt
1 tablespoon mustard
1 tablespoon horseradish sauce

1 To make the marinade, mix all the ingredients together in a shallow dish. Add the steaks and spoon the marinade over to coat evenly. Leave to marinate for 2-4 hours, turning occasionally.

2 For the garlic toast, mix the butter and garlic with seasoning to taste and spread on both sides of the bread.

3 To make the horseradish relish, mix the yogurt, mustard and horseradish sauce together in a bowl.

4 Lift the meat out of the marinade. Barbecue, basting occasionally with marinade, for 4-6 minutes each side, depending on the thickness of the steak and how you like your steak cooked.

5 Put the bread on the barbecue and toast for 1-2 minutes each side, until golden brown. Place a slice of garlic toast on each serving plate and top with a steak. Serve with the horseradish relish and a crisp green salad. *Serves 4.*

Steak with Gruyère

Charred steak with a tasty cheese filling, which melts deliciously if the steak is well done. A summer herb salad (page 46) makes an ideal accompaniment.

750g (1½lb) piece rump steak or
  2 sirloin steaks, about 4cm
  (1½ inches) thick
salt and pepper to taste
90g (3oz) gruyère cheese, grated

1 tablespoon coarse-grain
  mustard
2 cloves garlic, crushed
2 tablespoons olive oil
2 tablespoons red wine
few thyme sprigs

1 Make a horizontal slit through the lean edge of the steak to make a pocket, then season inside.
2 Mix the gruyère, mustard and 1 clove garlic together in a bowl, then use to fill the pocket and sew up.
3 For the marinade, mix the oil, wine, thyme and remaining garlic together in a shallow dish. Add the steak and spoon the marinade. Leave for 2 hours.
4 Lift the steak out of the marinade. Barbecue, basting occasionally with the marinade, for 5-10 minutes each side, depending how you like your steak cooked. To serve, cut the steak into 1cm (½ inch) slices. *Serves 4.*

Crusty Mustard Pork

3 tablespoons Meaux mustard
2 tablespoons natural yogurt
1 clove garlic, crushed
1 tablespoon olive oil

1 teaspoon clear honey
salt and pepper
4 boneless pork chops

1 Mix the mustard, yogurt, garlic, olive oil and honey together, with seasoning to taste.
2 Spread all over the chops to coat completely and barbecue for 10-15 minutes on each side, until crisp. Serve with nasturtium and apple salad (page 48). *Serves 4.*

Chorizo Sausages

These gorgeous Spanish sausages – heavily spiced with paprika and garlic – are usually sold cured and ready to eat. It's not easy to find the fresh variety, so try making your own – my family love them. You can buy sausage skins by the metre from your friendly butcher. One word of warning: these sausages contain no preservative, so they must be used on the day you make them or frozen until required.

375g (12oz) lean pork
125g (4oz) pork fat
125g (4oz) ground pork
1½ teaspoons salt
2 tablespoons paprika
¼ teaspoon black pepper
½ teaspoon ground cumin

½ teaspoon ground coriander
½ teaspoon sugar
¼ teaspoon chilli powder
2 cloves garlic, crushed
2 tablespoons red wine
1 metre sausage skin

1 Cut the lean pork and pork fat into 5mm (¼ inch) cubes and put into a bowl with the ground pork and all of the flavourings, including the wine.

2 Mix the ingredients together thoroughly with your hands, until evenly combined.

3 Run the tap through the sausage skin to moisten, then fix one end on to the base of a wide-necked funnel, with an elastic band. Put the mixture into the funnel and, using your fingers or the handle of a wooden spoon, press through into the skin until you have one long sausage. Twist the membrane every 10cm (4 inches) to make 8 sausage links.

4 Oil the sausages and barbecue for about 20 minutes, turning regularly until well browned. Serve with spiced beans (page 52) and a leafy green salad. *Makes 8 sausages.*

NOTE: If you haven't got a wide-necked funnel, use a plastic drink bottle. Cut the bottle in half using a sharp knife, rinse thoroughly and use the bottle neck as the funnel.

Chicken Tikka

I particularly like chicken cooked this way, but other meats are also good – notably lamb. A firm fleshed fish, such as halibut or swordfish, will also give excellent results. Naan bread, lemon wedges and an onion salad make ideal accompaniments.

4 boneless chicken breasts,
    about 625g (1¼lb) total
    weight
MARINADE:
3 cloves garlic, crushed
1cm (½ inch) piece fresh root
    (green) ginger, peeled and
    crushed
2 teaspoons ground coriander
1 teaspoon ground cinnamon
1 teaspoon ground cumin

1 teaspoon turmeric
1 tablespoon paprika
¼ teaspoon chilli powder
½ teaspoon salt
155ml (5 fl oz/⅔ cup) natural
    yogurt
2 tablespoons sunflower oil
juice of ½ lemon
TO SERVE:
lemon wedges

1 To make the marinade, mix the garlic, ginger, spices and salt together in a shallow dish. Add the yogurt, oil and lemon juice and mix well.

2 Cut the chicken into 2.5cm (1 inch) cubes, add to the marinade and turn to coat completely. Leave for about 2 hours.

3 Thread the pieces of chicken on to skewers and barbecue for 8-10 minutes, turning and brushing with more marinade occasionally. Serve with lemon wedges, naan bread and onion salad (below). *Serves 4.*

ONION SALAD: Slice 2 onions into thin rings, sprinkle with 4 tablespoons wine vinegar and 2 tablespoons chopped coriander leaves. Marinate for 30 minutes, turning occasionally.

Chicken Saté

Originating from Indonesia, satés are cubes of meat or fish, threaded on to sticks and cooked over charcoal. Any type of lean, tender meat or fish can be used. Peanut sauce is the traditional accompaniment: if you prefer you can replace the peanuts with crunchy peanut butter.

4 boneless chicken breasts,
skinned
MARINADE:
4 tablespoons soy sauce
2 cloves garlic, crushed
2 tablespoons lemon juice
1 tablespoon sesame oil
1 tablespoon clear honey

PEANUT SAUCE:
2 tablespoons sunflower oil
1 onion, chopped
2 cloves garlic, chopped
½ teaspoon chilli powder
1 teaspoon ground cumin
1 teaspoon ground coriander
1 teaspoon paprika
185ml (6 fl oz/¾ cup) water
125g (4oz/¾ cup) shelled
peanuts, finely ground

1 Cut the chicken into 2.5cm (1 inch) cubes and put into a shallow dish.

2 Mix all the marinade ingredients together in a bowl, then pour over the chicken, stir well to coat and leave to marinate for 2 hours.

3 Meanwhile make the peanut sauce. Heat the oil in a pan, add the onion and fry gently until softened. Add the garlic and spices and fry gently for 1 minute, then add the water. Stir in the ground peanuts, bring to the boil and cook, stirring, for 2 minutes. Remove from the heat.

4 Lift the chicken pieces out of the marinade and thread on to saté sticks. Add three quarters of the remaining marinade to the peanut sauce and thin with a little water if necessary. Reheat, then keep warm on the barbecue while cooking the saté.

5 Barbecue the saté for 3-4 minutes on each side, brushing frequently with the remaining marinade. Serve with the peanut sauce and yellow rice (page 24). *Serves 4.*

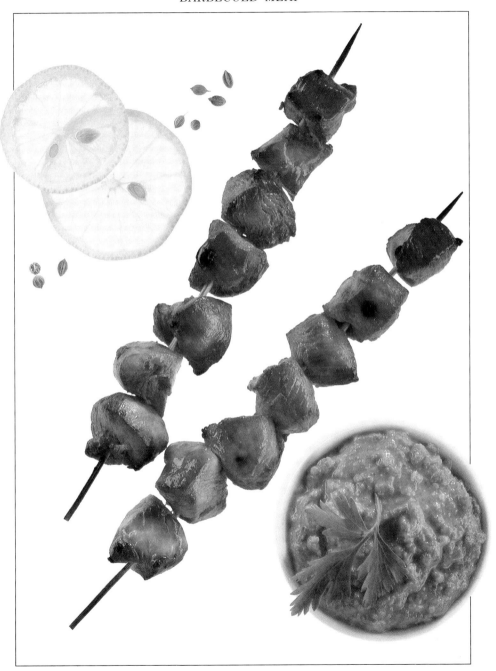

Poussins with Honey & Lemon

We first tasted charcoal-cooked chicken with honey and lemon in a tiny bay on the south coast of Turkey. The 'restaurant' owner was a great character who had only a charcoal fire, a clay oven and a deep freeze, set amongst the pine trees. He poured lemon juice and honey over everyone's chicken before retiring to his hammock to sleep under the stars!

2 poussins, about 625g (1¼lb) each
lemon wedges to serve
MARINADE:
3 tablespoons lemon juice

2 tablespoons clear honey
2 tablespoons olive oil
1 tablespoon chopped thyme
1 tablespoon chopped chives
salt and pepper to taste

1 With a sharp knife, split the poussins in half by cutting down through the breast bone, then each side of the backbone, discarding the backbone. Place in a shallow dish.

2 Mix all the marinade ingredients together in a bowl, then pour over the poussins and marinate for about 2 hours, turning occasionally.

3 Lift the poussins out of the marinade and barbecue for about 10-15 minutes each side, basting frequently and raising the barbecue rack if the coals become too hot.

4 Serve with lemon wedges and a pot of honey, so that everyone can help themselves to more if they wish!
Serves 4.

DEVILLED POUSSINS: Omit the marinade. Combine 4 tablespoons each of tomato ketchup and fruit sauce with 1 tablespoon each of soy sauce, Worcestershire sauce, clear honey and Dijon mustard; mix until thoroughly blended. Brush all over the poussins and cook as above, basting with extra sauce. Serve with yellow rice (page 24) and a green salad.

DEVILLED DRUMSTICKS: Make 2 deep cuts in each drumstick, brush liberally with devilled sauce (as for devilled poussins) and cook for 15 minutes, turning frequently.

Stuffed Duck Breasts

Served with a tangy blackberry sauce, barbecued duck breasts are
quite delicious.

4 boned duck breasts
oil for brushing
STUFFING:
2 tablespoons olive oil
1 onion, chopped
1 dessert apple, chopped
30g (1oz/½ cup) wholemeal
* breadcrumbs*
15g (½oz/2 tablespoons)
* chopped hazelnuts, toasted*
1 teaspoon chopped thyme
1 teaspoon chopped lemon balm

salt and pepper to taste
BLACKBERRY SAUCE:
125g (4oz) blackberries
60ml (2 fl oz/¼ cup) port
60ml (2 fl oz/¼ cup) apple juice
4 spring onions (green shallots),
* sliced*
1 teaspoon chopped thyme
2 teaspoons arrowroot
1 tablespoon water
1 teaspoon clear honey

1 Make a deep horizontal cut in each duck breast to form a
pocket.
2 To make the stuffing, heat the oil in a pan, add the onion
and apple and fry gently for 5 minutes until softened.
Transfer to a bowl, add the remaining ingredients and mix
thoroughly. Spoon the stuffing into the duck breast pockets
and secure the openings with saté sticks.
3 To make the sauce, put the blackberries, port, apple juice,
spring onions (shallots) and thyme into a saucepan, cover
and cook gently for 5 minutes. Blend the arrowroot with the
water until smooth, then add to the sauce with the honey
and cook gently, stirring, until thickened. Transfer to the
side of the barbecue and keep warm.
4 Push the coals slightly away from the centre of the
barbecue and lay a small foil tray in the middle, to catch the
dripping fat and prevent the fire flaring.
5 Lay duck breasts, skin side down, on the barbecue grid
and cook for 15-20 minutes; there is no need to baste as the
skin is naturally fatty. Turn the duck breasts, brush with a
little oil and cook for 10-15 minutes, depending on size, until
tender. Serve with the blackberry sauce. *Serves 4.*

Vegetable Kebabs

Few barbecue recipes appeal to vegetarians – here's one that does. It makes an excellent accompaniment too.

A rosemary brush is ideal for basting the kebabs and imparts a delicate flavour – tie a few sprigs of rosemary together, twining string around the stalks to make the handle.

375g (12oz) aubergines
  (eggplants), preferably small
  pink ones
salt and pepper to taste
500g (1lb) baby new potatoes
1 red pepper
4 small onions
125ml (4 fl oz/½ cup) olive oil
1 clove garlic, finely chopped
125g (4oz) button mushrooms
8 bay leaves

WATERCRESS DRESSING:
1 bunch watercress, chopped
1 clove garlic
1 teaspoon clear honey
1 tablespoon lemon juice
2 spring onions (green shallots),
  chopped
90ml (3 fl oz/⅓ cup) natural
  yogurt
90ml (3 fl oz/⅓ cup) thick
  mayonnaise

1 Cut the aubergines (eggplants) into 2.5cm (1 inch) pieces and put into a colander. Sprinkle with salt and leave to drain for 30 minutes. Rinse and pat dry with absorbent kitchen paper.

2 Cook the potatoes in boiling salted water for 10 minutes until tender; drain. Halve and seed the red pepper, then cut into squares. Cut the onions into quarters.

3 Put the oil and garlic into a bowl, add the aubergine (eggplant) and mushrooms and turn until evenly coated.

4 Thread the aubergine (eggplant), onions, mushrooms, pepper, potatoes and bay leaves alternately on to 8 large skewers. Brush thoroughly with the remaining oil and garlic.

5 To make the watercress dressing, put all the ingredients except the mayonnaise in a blender or food processor and work to a purée. Fold into the mayonnaise until smooth.

6 Barbecue the kebabs for 10-15 minutes, turning occasionally and basting frequently with oil. Serve with the watercress dressing. *Serves 4 or 8.*

Charcoal-Grilled Vegetables

These have a smokey flavour – delicious with savoury butters.

VEGETABLES:
baking potatoes
aubergines (eggplants)
corn-on-the-cob
small onions
red, green and yellow peppers
whole garlic bulbs

FLAVOURED BUTTERS:
125g (4oz) butter, softened
salt and pepper to taste
squeeze of lemon juice
3 tablespoons chopped herbs, eg:
chives, parsley, thyme, fennel,
chervil, tarragon or dill

POTATOES: Cut a deep cross on each potato and insert a few slivers of garlic if you like. Wrap in a double thickness of foil and place in the embers for 45 minutes to 1 hour. Unwrap, press to open up the cross and add a knob of herb butter.

AUBERGINES (EGGPLANTS): Cut into 1cm (½ inch) slices, sprinkle with salt and leave for 30 minutes. Rinse and pat dry with absorbent kitchen paper. Brush generously with olive oil, season and barbecue for 3-5 minutes each side.

CORN-ON-THE-COB: Remove as much silk as possible from the corn, but leave covered by the husk. Barbecue for about 20 minutes, turning frequently. Peel back the husk and serve the succulent sweetcorn with herb butter.

ONIONS: Cut onions into quarters and thread on to skewers. Brush generously with olive oil, then barbecue for 10-15 minutes, turning once, until golden to dark brown.

PEPPERS: Halve and seed the peppers, brush with olive oil and barbecue for 15-20 minutes, turning once. Or thread pepper squares on to skewers, brush with olive oil and barbecue for 10-15 minutes, turning occasionally.

GARLIC: Place whole heads of garlic in the embers for 8-10 minutes, until the skin splits. The flesh will be soft, creamy and surprisingly mild in flavour.

FLAVOURED BUTTERS: Mix the softened butter with seasoning and lemon juice until smooth. Add the herbs, and mix until evenly blended. For garlic butter, add 2 crushed garlic cloves (omitting the herbs if you prefer).

Cheese Wrapped in Vine Leaves

Cheese is delicious cooked on the barbecue, but it needs to be protected from the heat. Vine leaves are ideal wrappings; they also impart an excellent sharp flavour. These little parcels are particularly good cooked quickly over very hot coals, so that the leaves char and crispen, before the cheese overcooks.

Other cheeses that work well are fontina, raclette, emmenthal and crottin de chavignol. These cheese parcels are ideal to serve vegetarians, or as appetizing nibbles before the main course.

100g (3½oz) roll goat's cheese
185g (6oz) gruyère cheese

½ x 227g (8oz) packet preserved
vine leaves
olive oil for brushing

1 Cut the goat's cheese into 2 equal rounds, then cut each round into quarters, giving 8 pieces. Cut the gruyère into 2cm (¾ inch) cubes.

2 Rinse the vine leaves under running cold water to remove excess salt; drain and pat dry with absorbent kitchen paper. Cut larger vine leaves in half.

3 Lay the vine leaves out on a work surface and place a piece of goat's cheese or gruyère on each one. Fold the vine leaves over the filling to enclose. Carefully thread the parcels on to wooden kebab skewers, securing the openings as you do so; put about 3 parcels on each skewer.

4 Brush with oil and barbecue for 3-5 minutes, until the leaves are crisp and the cheese is just beginning to melt. Serve immediately. *Serves 4 or 8.*

Summer Herb Salad

A basic green salad with a variety of flavouring ingredients, depending on what's available. I love using rocket, which is very easy to grow, and has a wonderful, warm, peppery flavour. There are other interesting additions, such as nasturtium leaves which also have a peppery flavour; sorrel which has a sharp tang – so you don't need too much; young dandelion leaves; flat leafed parsley – stronger than ordinary parsley; basil or watercress. If frisée (curly endive) is not available, use any other crisp lettuce instead. Flowers also give interest, colour and sweetness to a salad. I particularly like chive flowers, violas, nasturtiums and marigolds.

½ head frisée (endive)
few radicchio leaves
2 heads chicory (witlof), sliced
*   diagonally*
handful of lamb's lettuce leaves
*   (corn salad)*
handful of rocket leaves
handful of nasturtium leaves
few small edible flowers
*   (optional)*

DRESSING:
3 tablespoons olive oil
1 tablespoon cider vinegar
1 teaspoon French mustard
1 clove garlic, crushed
1 teaspoon clear honey
salt and pepper to taste

1 Tear the frisée (endive) and radicchio into pieces and place in a bowl with the chicory (witlof), lamb's lettuce (corn salad), rocket and nasturtium leaves.

2 Whisk all the dressing ingredients together in a small bowl, or shake in a screw-topped jar until evenly combined.

3 Pour the dressing over the salad just before serving, toss thoroughly and scatter the flowers over the top. *Serves 4-6.*

Nasturtium & Apple Salad

Both the leaves and flowers of nasturtiums are excellent in salads. The leaves have a peppery flavour, while the flowers are sweet, so they complement each other well.

3 red-skinned apples, cored
24 nasturtium leaves
DRESSING:
3 tablespoons olive oil
1 tablespoon lemon juice
1 teaspoon clear honey
salt and pepper to taste
TO GARNISH:
8 nasturtium flowers
1 tablespoon sesame seeds,
   toasted

1 For the dressing, put all the ingredients in a screw-topped jar and shake vigorously to combine.
2 Slice the apples thinly into a bowl. Add the nasturtium leaves, pour over the dressing and toss well.
3 Transfer to a salad bowl, arrange the flowers on top and sprinkle with sesame seeds. *Serves 4.*

Chicory & Avocado Salad

1 avocado
6 rashers streaky bacon, rinds
   removed, chopped
3 heads chicory (witlof), sliced
   diagonally
60g (2oz/¹/₂ cup) hazelnuts,
   chopped and toasted
2 tablespoons chopped chives
DRESSING:
3 tablespoons hazelnut oil
1 tablespoon cider vinegar
1 teaspoon Dijon mustard
1 clove garlic, crushed
salt and pepper to taste

1 For the dressing, put all the ingredients in a screw-topped jar and shake vigorously to combine.
2 Halve, stone and peel the avocado. Slice into a bowl and pour over the dressing, tossing until well coated.
3 Fry the bacon in its own fat until crisp, the add to the bowl with the chicory (witlof), hazelnuts and chives. Stir gently until evenly mixed. *Serves 4.*

Tomato, Cucumber & Onion Salad

This accompaniment is perfect served in pitta packets.

4 tomatoes, roughly chopped
½ cucumber, chopped
1 small onion, finely chopped
2 tablespoons chopped parsley

DRESSING:
3 tablespoons olive oil
1 tablespoon cider vinegar
1 clove garlic, crushed
½ teaspoon clear honey
salt and pepper to taste

1 Combine the salad ingredients in a bowl.
2 Shake the dressing ingredients together in a screw-topped jar until thoroughly blended. Pour over the salad and toss well. *Serves 4.*

Oriental Salad

This salad is ideal to serve with satays or beef teryaki.

125g (4oz) mange tout (snow
*   peas), topped and tailed*
125g (4oz) baby corn cobs
1 small red pepper, seeded and
*   sliced*
125g (4oz) button mushrooms,
*   quartered*
125g (4oz) bean sprouts
3 spring onions (green shallots),
*   sliced diagonally*

2 tablespoons sesame seeds,
*   toasted*
SESAME DRESSING:
2 tablespoons tahini (sesame
*   seed paste)*
2 tablespoons rice wine vinegar
2 tablespoons medium sherry
1 tablespoon sesame oil
2 tablespoons soy sauce
1 clove garlic, crushed

1 Blanch the mange tout (snow peas) and corn cobs in boiling water for 2 minutes, rinse in cold water, then drain. Halve the corn cobs diagonally.
2 Place all the salad ingredients in a serving bowl.
3 To make the sesame dressing, put the tahini in a small bowl and gradually mix in the vinegar and sherry; it will thicken at first, becoming thinner as you add more liquid.
4 Pour the dressing over the salad and toss well. *Serves 4.*

Ratatouille

1 aubergine (eggplant)
salt and pepper to taste
6 tablespoons olive oil
2 cloves garlic, chopped
250g (8oz) courgettes (zucchini),
  sliced

1 onion, sliced
1 red and 1 green pepper, seeded
  and sliced
500g (1lb) tomatoes, skinned
  and cut into wedges
2 tablespoons chopped parsley

1 Slice the aubergine (eggplant), put into a colander, sprinkle with salt and leave for 30 minutes. Rinse and dry with absorbent kitchen paper.
2 Heat half the oil in a frying pan and fry the aubergine (eggplant) slices in batches until pale golden brown, adding more oil as necessary. Drain on kitchen paper.
3 Add the remaining oil to the pan and fry the garlic, courgettes (zucchini), onion and peppers for 10-15 minutes, stirring occasionally, until softened. Add the tomatoes and aubergine (eggplant), season and cook for 5 minutes.
4 Stir in the parsley. Serve hot or cold. *Serves 4.*

Spiced Beans

2 tablespoons oil
1 onion, chopped
1 stick celery, chopped
2 cloves garlic, chopped
1 teaspoon paprika
1/4-1/2 teaspoon chilli powder
1 tablespoon tomato purée (paste)

440g (14oz) can chopped
  tomatoes
salt to taste
2 x 440g (14oz) cans red kidney
  beans or pinto beans, drained
2 tablespoons chopped parsley
3 tomatoes, chopped (optional)

1 Heat the oil in a large pan, add the onion and celery and fry until softened.
2 Add the garlic, paprika and chilli powder if using, and fry for a further 1 minute. Add the tomato purée (paste), tomatoes and salt, cover and cook for 10 minutes.
3 Add the kidney beans or pinto beans and parsley. Cover and cook for 5 minutes, then serve. If serving cold, allow to cool, then add the tomatoes. *Serves 4.*

Spicy Stuffed Tomatoes

2 beefsteak tomatoes	1 teaspoon ground cumin
2 tablespoons oil	2 tablespoons currants
1 onion, chopped	2 tablespoons chopped parsley
2 tablespoons pine nuts	125g (4oz/³⁄4 cup) cooked rice
2 cloves garlic, chopped	parsley sprigs to garnish

1 Preheat the oven to 180C (350F/Gas 4). Cut the tomatoes in half, scoop out the pulp with a spoon, chop and set aside. Turn the tomatoes upside down to drain.

2 Heat the oil in a frying pan, add the onion and cook until softened. Add the pine nuts and garlic and cook for 1 minute. Stir in the cumin, then add the currants, parsley and rice with the tomato pulp; stir well.

3 Spoon the mixture into the tomato halves and place in a greased shallow dish. Bake in the oven for 20 minutes. Garnish with parsley to serve. *Serves 4.*

Gratin Dauphinois

Like the stuffed tomatoes above, this is a useful accompaniment to prepare in advance, especially if space on the barbecue is limited.

30g (1oz) butter	2 cloves garlic, finely chopped
750g (1¹⁄2lb) potatoes	315ml (10 fl oz/1¹⁄4 cups) double
salt and pepper	(thick) cream

1 Preheat the oven to 190C (375F/Gas 5). Grease a shallow ovenproof dish liberally with half of the butter.

2 Slice the potatoes thinly and arrange in the dish, sprinkling salt, pepper and garlic between each layer.

3 Pour over the cream to three-quarters fill the dish and dot with the remaining butter. Bake in the oven for about 1¹⁄2 hours, until golden brown on top. *Serves 6.*

Seafood Platter

When we go to Brittany it is our first priority to eat an 'assiette des fruits de mer', at out favourite restaurant on the quayside. Eaten with lots of French bread, mayonnaise and a bottle of Muscadet, its a wonderful way to spend a few hours.

4 small crabs, cooked
60g (2oz/1 cup) fresh
  breadcrumbs
1-2 tablespoons lemon juice
2 tablespoons single (light)
  cream
salt and pepper to taste
8 langoustines, cooked

625ml (1 pint/2½ cups) winkles,
  cooked
8 oysters
625ml (1 pint/2½ cups) prawns,
  cooked
edible seaweed or lettuce leaves
  to serve (optional)
lemon wedges to garnish

1 Clean the crabs with a damp cloth and twist off the claws and legs. Crack the claws with nutcrackers; set aside.
2 To remove the shells, place the tail flap towards you. Hold the shell firmly with your fingers and, using your thumbs, push the body firmly upwards until it loosens, then lift the body off the shell.
3 Remove and discard the stomach sac from behind the eyes in the shell. Scoop the brown meat from the shells into a small bowl and add the breadcrumbs, lemon juice, cream and seasoning; mix with a fork then transfer to 4 small serving bowls.
4 Remove and discard the grey feathery gills, or 'dead mens fingers' from the body. Cut the body in half, using a sharp heavy knife, so that the edible meat is more accessible.
5 Line 4 individual serving platters with seaweed or lettuce leaves if desired. Position the langoustines and bowls of crab meat in the centre of each platter. Arrange the winkles, oysters, prawns, crab claws, legs and body around the edge. Garnish with lemon wedges.
6 Serve with plain mayonnaise or tomato mayonnaise (page 58) and plenty of French bread. Provide each guest with a crab pick, finger bowl and a large napkin! *Serves 4.*

Poached Salmon Trout

Salmon trout or sea trout has a delicate flavour and is less rich than salmon. The flesh is pale pink in colour, and at its best during the summer months. You will need a fish kettle to cook the fish; you should be able to borrow one from your fishmonger if necessary.

1.75-2kg (3½-4lb) sea trout,
  cleaned
1 bouquet garni
1 lemon, sliced
12 peppercorns
1 tablespoon sea salt
TO GARNISH:
24 whole cooked prawns
fennel sprigs
cucumber slices

TOMATO MAYONNAISE:
3 tomatoes, skinned, seeded and
  chopped
1 clove garlic, crushed
1 teaspoon caster sugar
1 tablespoon tomato purée
  (paste)
315ml (10 fl oz/1¼ cups)
  mayonnaise

1 Wash the fish, cut off the fins and cut the centre of the tail into a sharp V shape.
2 Place the fish in a fish kettle, curling it to fit if necessary. Add the bouquet garni, lemon, peppercorns and salt, then pour in enough water to just cover the fish.
3 Bring to the boil very slowly: it should take 40 minutes to reach a simmer. As soon as the surface breaks into a simmer, turn off the heat, cover and let cool overnight.
4 To make the tomato mayonnaise, put the tomatoes, garlic, sugar and tomato purée (paste) in a blender or food processor and work to a purée. Gradually stir into the mayonnaise, then transfer to a serving dish.
5 Lift the fish out of the liquid on to a piece of absorbent kitchen paper placed on a pad of newspaper. Snip the skin behind the head and all along the backbone, then carefully peel away from the fish. Remove the fin bones.
6 Carefully lift the fish on to a serving platter, using two fish slices. Garnish with the prawns, fennel and cucumber slices. Serve with tomato mayonnaise, cucumber salad (page 10) and new potatoes. *Serves 8.*

Shellfish Salad

Queen scallops – the tiny ones which are usually cheaper than ordinary scallops – can be used whole for this recipe instead of the familiar larger ones; you will need approximately 250g (8oz) in weight. The shellfish cooking liquor makes an excellent base for a fish soup, so I usually freeze this for later use.

8 shelled scallops, cleaned
500g (1lb) mussels
1 avocado
375g (12oz) peeled prawns
2 tomatoes, skinned and cut into
  strips
250g (8oz/1½ cups) cooked rice
2 tablespoons chopped chives
2 tablespoons chopped chervil

LEMON DRESSING:
4 tablespoons olive oil
2 tablespoons lemon juice
1 clove garlic, crushed
salt and pepper to taste
TO GARNISH:
dill sprigs

1 Put the scallops into a pan, add sufficient water to three-quarters cover them and bring almost to the boil. Simmer gently for 2 minutes, then leave to cool. Drain, then cut each scallop into 3 pieces.
2 To clean the mussels, scrub them thoroughly under cold running water, removing the beards and discarding any mussels which stay open when tapped.
3 Bring 155ml (5 fl oz/⅔ cup) water to the boil in a large pan. Add the mussels, cover and cook briskly, shaking the pan occasionally, for 2-3 minutes until the shells open; discard any that remain closed. Cool slightly, then remove the mussels from their shells.
4 To make the dressing, put all the ingredients in a screw-topped jar and shake vigorously to combine.
5 Halve, stone and peel the avocado, then cut into chunks.
6 Combine the shelled mussels, scallops, prawns, tomatoes avocado, rice and herbs in a bowl. Pour over the salad dressing and toss gently. Leave for about 1 hour before serving to allow the flavours to mingle. To serve, garnish with dill. *Serves 4.*

Boned Chicken with Tarragon

Not as difficult to do as it sounds, and of course the chicken can be prepared and cooked the day before you serve it.

1 chicken, weighing about 2kg (4lb)
125g (4oz/½ cup) ricotta or curd cheese
2 cloves garlic, crushed

2 tablespoons chopped parsley
2 tablespoons chopped chives
1 tablespoon chopped tarragon
½ egg, beaten
salt and pepper to taste

1 To bone the chicken, cut the skin down the centre of the back. Carefully scrape flesh away from carcass, using a small knife. When you reach the leg joint, cut through it.

2 Holding the end of the leg bone in one hand, cut away the flesh and scrape the thigh bone clean. Continue clearing the drumstick until the whole leg bone is free of flesh, then cut through the knuckle and pull the bone out, turning it inside out. Repeat with the other leg.

3 Break wing joint and cut free from carcass. Scrape flesh away along wing bone, cut off the pinion, and pull bone free from flesh. Repeat with the other wing.

4 Continue working down either side of the breast bone. Finally work flesh away from the breast bone, taking care to avoid puncturing the skin, and remove carcass.

5 To make the stuffing, mix the cheese with the garlic, herbs, egg and seasoning.

6 Preheat the oven to 190C (375F/Gas 5). Open out the chicken, tuck in the wing flesh and spread the stuffing on top. Roll up and sew together, using a trussing needle and cotton string. Tie neatly at 2.5cm (1 inch) intervals.

7 Brush with olive oil and sprinkle with salt and pepper. Place the chicken in a roasting tin and cover with foil. Bake in the preheated oven for 1 hour, basting occasionally. Remove foil and cook for a further 15 minutes, until the skin is golden brown and the juices run clear when the meat is pierced with a sharp knife. Allow to cool, remove string and carve. Serve with new potatoes and a salad. *Serves 6.*

Chicken & Asparagus Salad

A delicious summer salad flavoured with fresh tarragon and pine nuts. When asparagus is not in season, you can replace it with sliced avocado. I like to serve this salad with new potatoes and a crisp green salad.

350g (12oz) asparagus spears
350g (12oz) cooked chicken
TARRAGON DRESSING:
1 tablespoon tarragon vinegar
2 teaspoons clear honey

1 tablespoon chopped tarragon
salt and pepper
4 rashers streaky bacon, rinds
  removed
2 tablespoons pine nuts, toasted

1 To prepare the asparagus, bend the lower end of the stalks until they snap. The stalks will break at the point where they become tough; discard the woody ends. Cut the asparagus into 4cm (1½ inch) lengths, keeping the tips separate. Cook the stalks for 3 minutes in boiling salted water, add the tips and cook for a further 3 minutes until just tender. Drain and rinse in cold water; drain.
2 Cut the chicken into 2.5cm (1 inch) strips and place in a bowl with the asparagus.
3 To make the dressing, mix all the ingredients together in a small bowl, then pour over the chicken and asparagus. Toss gently until evenly coated. Transfer to a serving dish.
4 Chop the bacon roughly and fry in its own fat until crisp. Scatter the bacon and pine nuts over the salad to serve.
Serves 4.

NOTE: Chilled soups make excellent starters for patio meals, as they can be prepared well ahead. For dessert, I generally like to serve simple fruity concoctions; for suggestions see pages 70-74.

Salade Tiède

A wonderful salad when you want to serve something quick and easy, but also rather special. Everything can be prepared early in the day, before the sun tempts you into the garden. Only the croûtons, bacon and mushrooms need to be cooked just before you're ready to eat. Serve with plenty of warm baguettes.

½ frisée (curly endive)
1 oak leaf lettuce or mignonette
25g (1oz) lamb's lettuce (corn
*   salad) or purslane*
few radicchio leaves
handful of rocket leaves
2 heads chicory (witlof), sliced
*   diagonally*
4 tablespoons olive oil
1 clove garlic, halved

2 slices bread, cut into cubes
185g (6oz) wild mushrooms,
*   such as ceps, chanterelles or*
*   field mushrooms*
125g (4oz) smoked bacon, rinds
*   removed, cut into strips*
2 tablespoons raspberry wine
*   vinegar*
salt and pepper to taste
few chives to garnish

1 Prepare all the salad leaves, tearing the frisée (endive) and larger leaves into smaller pieces. Place in a salad bowl and toss gently.

2 Heat the oil in a frying pan, add the garlic and bread cubes and fry until crisp and golden. Remove the bread cubes from the pan and keep warm.

3 Add the mushrooms and bacon to the pan and fry quickly for 5-6 minutes, stirring frequently, then remove with a slotted spoon and scatter over the salad. Discard the garlic.

4 Quickly pour the vinegar into the pan, stir to mix in the juices, then pour over the salad. Season well with salt and pepper and sprinkle with the croûtons. Garnish with chives to serve. *Serves 4.*

VARIATION: Replace the mushrooms with 185g (6oz) chicken livers. Fry with the bacon for 6-7 minutes, until tender but still slightly pink inside. Thinly slice after frying and scatter over the salad. Continue as above.

Crudités, Aioli & Bagna Cauda

Colourful, crisp crudités served with two dipping sauces from the Mediterranean: bagna cauda from Italy and aioli from Provence. Use only the freshest young vegetables for crudités – select any varieties that are in season – and provide lots of French bread for mopping up the bagna cauda.

12 -16 thin asparagus spears
250g (8oz) broccoli or
  cauliflower florets
1 bunch baby new carrots
1 bunch radishes
1 bunch spring onions (green
  shallots)
125g (4oz) button mushrooms,
  halved
2 heads chicory (witlof),
  separated into leaves
375g (12oz) new potatoes, boiled
1 red pepper, seeded and cut
  into strips

AIOLI:
2 egg yolks
6 cloves garlic, crushed
½ teaspoon salt
315ml (10 fl oz/1¼ cups) olive
  oil
2 teaspoons lemon juice
BAGNA CAUDA:
155ml (¼ pint/⅔ cup) olive oil
6 cloves garlic, chopped
50g (1¾oz) can anchovies,
  drained and finely chopped
90g (3oz) butter
pepper to taste

1 Blanch the asparagus and broccoli, or cauliflower, separately in boiling salted water for 2 minutes, drain. Arrange all the vegetables on a serving platter.
2 To make the aioli, beat the egg yolks with the garlic and salt until thickened. Add the oil a little at a time, beating continuously. As the mixture thickens, add 1 teaspoon lemon juice, then add the remaining oil in a steady stream, beating vigorously. Add the remaining lemon juice and mix thoroughly. Transfer to a serving dish.
3 To make the bagna cauda, heat the oil in an earthenware pot, add the garlic and anchovies and cook, stirring, over a low heat for 4-5 minutes, until the anchovies almost dissolve. Add the butter and stir until melted. Season with pepper. Keep dish warm at the table over a candle burner.
4 Serve the crudités with the aioli and bagna cauda, together with plenty of crusty bread. *Serves 8.*

Tropical Fruit Kebabs

These are delicious served hot, if your embers are still burning. If not the kebabs can be served just as they are.

1 papaya (paw-paw)　　　　　*2 kiwi fruit, peeled*
2 bananas　　　　　　　　　*2 tablespoons clear honey*
2 slices pineapple　　　　　*lemon balm sprigs to decorate*

1 Peel, halve and deseed the papaya (paw-paw), then cut into cubes. Slice the bananas thickly. Remove skin and core from the pineapple, then cut into chunks. Halve the kiwi fruit and cut each half into 4 chunks. Thread the fruit alternately onto 8 skewers.
2 Trickle the honey over the fruit kebabs, using a fork. Barbecue for 5-10 minutes, depending on the heat of the embers, turning occasionally. *Serves 4.*

Barbecued Bananas

By the time the main course has been cooked and devoured, the embers are usually still hot, so why not make use of them for a barbecued dessert with a Caribbean flavour!

4 bananas　　　　　　　　　*2 tablespoons rum*
1 tablespoon demerara sugar

1 Cut out a thin slice of skin along the length of the banana, loosen the skin slightly and mark criss-crosses in the flesh.
2 Sprinkle a little sugar over the banana flesh, then moisten with the rum.
3 Lay the bananas on the grid, cut side uppermost, and cook for 5-15 minutes, depending on the intensity of the heat. Alternatively, you can lay the bananas directly on the embers, in which case they will cook quickly. *Serves 4.*

Summer Strawberry Whirl

*500g (1lb) strawberries, hulled
and halved
1 tablespoon icing sugar, sifted
2 tablespoons Grand Marnier*

*185ml (6 fl oz/³/₄ cup) double
(thick) cream
155ml (5 fl oz/²/₃ cup) fromage
frais*

1 Put half of the strawberries in a blender or food processor with the icing sugar and blend until smooth. Sieve to remove pips, then stir in the liqueur.
2 Whip the cream until it holds its shape, then fold in the fromage frais and all but 6 of the remaining strawberries.
3 Lightly fold in the strawberry purée and serve decorated with the remaining strawberries. *Serves 4-6.*

Kir & Currant Chartreuse

A lovely summer dessert to serve when red currants and black-currants are in season; when they are not use strawberries instead, and substitute liqueur de framboise for the cassis.

*315ml (10 fl oz/1¹/₄ cups) sweet
white wine
15g (¹/₂oz) gelatine
2 tablespoons clear honey*

*125g (4oz) red currants
125g (4oz) blackcurrants
125g (4oz) raspberries
3 tablespoons cassis*

1 Put 3 tablespoons wine in a cup, sprinkle over the gelatine and leave to soak for 5 minutes.
2 Put remaining wine in a saucepan with the honey, red and blackcurrants. Bring to the boil and simmer gently for 5 minutes. Remove from heat, add gelatine and stir until dissolved. Add raspberries and liqueur and leave to cool.
3 When the jelly is on the point of setting, pour into a 500g (1lb) loaf tin and chill until set.
4 To turn out, briefly dip the tin into hot water and invert on to a serving plate. Cut into slices and serve with whipped cream. *Serves 6.*

Summer Fruit Fool

A 'fool' is really just a mixture of fruit purée and cream. You can make it less rich by replacing some of the cream with yogurt or fromage frais. Any seasonal fruits can be used – fresh soft fruits, such as raspberries or strawberries – or stewed gooseberries, apricots or rhubarb.

Serve fools simply in glass dishes, or more elegantly in these tuile baskets.

TUILE BASKETS:
30g (1oz/¼ cup) plain flour
60g (2oz/¼ cup) caster sugar
1 egg white
30g (1oz) butter, melted
TO DECORATE:
strawberry or raspberry leaves

FOOL:
315g (10oz) summer fruits, such
as strawberries, raspberries
etc.
60g (2oz/¼ cup) caster sugar
315ml (10 fl oz/1¼ cups) double
(thick) cream

1 To make the baskets, preheat the oven to 190C (375F/Gas 5). Grease and flour 2 or 3 baking sheets. Mix the flour and sugar together in a bowl, add the egg white and melted butter, then beat thoroughly until smooth.

2 Place 7 spoonfuls of the mixture, well apart, on the baking sheets; spread thinly to 13cm (5 inch) rounds.

3 Bake one tray at a time for 6-7 minutes, until golden round the edges. Leave to cool slightly, then carefully remove each biscuit with a sharp knife and place top side down over the base of an inverted glass. Mould each biscuit to form a basket with wavy edges. Hold in position until set, then carefully remove. (As the mixture will make 7 tuiles, this allows for a breakage.)

4 To make the fool, put the fruit into a blender or food processor with the sugar and blend to a purée. Press through a nylon sieve to remove pips.

5 Whip the cream until it holds its shape firmly, then fold in the fruit purée. Spoon into the tuile baskets and decorate with strawberry or raspberry leaves. *Serves 6.*

Strawberry Sparkle

A refreshing summer drink, perfect as a barbecue aperitif.

250g (8oz) strawberries, hulled
2 tablespoons caster sugar
juice of 1 orange

crushed ice to serve
750ml (24 fl oz/3 cups) demi-sec
sparkling wine

1 Put the strawberries, sugar and orange juice into a food processor or blender and blend to a purée. Press through a nylon sieve to remove the pips.
2 Pour into champagne glasses, add crushed ice and top up with the sparkling wine. *Serves 8.*

Watermelon Crush

A refreshing, virtually non-alcoholic drink for a hot summer day, although you can replace the water with a dry white wine if you prefer. To frost the glasses, dip the rims into egg white, then into caster sugar and set aside while preparing the drink.

375g (12oz) watermelon, skin
and seeds removed
2 tablespoons cassis
375ml (12 fl oz/1½ cups)
lemonade

375ml (12 fl oz/1½ cups)
sparkling mineral water
TO SERVE:
crushed ice
lemon balm sprigs

1 Cut the watermelon into chunks and place in a food processor or blender. Work until smooth.
2 Pour into a jug and stir in the cassis. Add the lemonade and mineral water.
3 Pour into glasses and top up with crushed ice. Decorate with lemon balm sprigs. *Serves 8.*

NOTE: Other suitable drinks to accompany barbecues and *al fresco* meals include Champagne, sparkling Saumur, Kir or Pimm's.

Elderflower Champagne

Without doubt my favourite drink. The fragrant aroma and delicate taste epitomise summer, and its not even alcoholic! The elderflower season is short – May and June – so catch it while you can. Pick the creamy heads when they have just come into flower.

4 large heads elderflower
pared rind and juice of 1 lemon
3 tablespoons white wine
vinegar

750g (1½lb/3¾ cups) caster
sugar
5 litres (1 gallon/20 cups) water

1 Put all the ingredients together in a clean bucket, stir well, cover and leave for 24 hours.
2 Strain through muslin, then pour into very strong clean screw-topped bottles. Leave in a cool place for at least 2 weeks before drinking. *Makes about 6 litres (10 pints).*

NOTE: Elderflower champagne will keep up to 2 months but pressure is liable to build up in the bottles and may need to be released a little after 2-3 weeks. Check periodically: unchecked bottles may explode.

Elderflower Cordial

Simply mix with sparkling mineral water or a sparkling wine for a delicious summer drink, or add to fruit salads.

pared rind and juice of 2 lemons
625ml (1 pint/2½ cups) water

500g (1lb/2½ cups) caster sugar
8 heads elderflower

1 Put the lemon rind and juice, water and sugar into a pan and bring to the boil, stirring to dissolve the sugar. Add the elderflowers and simmer for 15 minutes; cool.
2 Strain through muslin, then pour into small clean screw-topped glass bottles. *Makes 1 litre (38 fl oz/5 cups).*

NOTE: If the cordial is to be kept, the bottles must be sterilized by submerging in boiling water for 15 minutes.

Index

Aïoli 68

Bagna cauda 68
Bananas, barbecued 70
Beans, spiced 52
Beef:
  Beef teriyaki 24
  Fillet steak on garlic toast 26
  Homemade burgers 20
  Mexican marinated beef 22
  Steak with gruyère 28
Butters, flavoured 40

Cheese wrapped in vine leaves 44
Chicken:
  Boned chicken with tarragon 62
  Chicken and asparagus salad 64
  Chicken saté 34
  Chicken tikka 32
  Devilled drumsticks 36
  Devilled poussins 36
  Poussins with honey and lemon 36
  Spit roast chicken with
    tarragon 18
Chicory and avocado salad 48
Crudités 68
Cucumber:
  Caçik 16
  Cucumber salad 10

Duck breasts, stuffed 38

Elderflower champagne 78
Elderflower cordial 78

Fish:
  Barbecued fish with fennel 10
  Barbecued fish steaks 8
  Herby fish kebabs 8
  Spiced fish kebabs 8
Flower pot barbecue 12
Fruit fool 74

Garlic bread 12
Gratin dauphinois 54

Halibut steaks, marinated 12

Kir and currant chartreuse 72

Lamb:
  Adana kebab 16
  Mini kebabs 16
  Sis kebab 14
  Spit roast lamb 18
  Yogurtlu kebab 14

Nasturtium and apple salad 48

Onion salad 32
Oriental salad 50

Pork:
  Chorizo sausages 30
  Crusty mustard pork 28
Prawns, barbecued 4

Ratatouille 52
Rice, yellow fried 24

Salade tiède 66
Salmon brochettes 6
Salmon trout, poached 58
Sardines, Spanish 4
Scallop and bacon kebabs 6
Seafood platter 56
Shellfish salad 60
Strawberry sparkle 76
Strawberry whirl 72
Summer herb salad 46

Tomato, cucumber and onion salad
  50
Tomatoes, spicy stuffed 54
Tropical fruit kebabs 70

Vegetable kebabs 42
Vegetables, charcoal-grilled 40
Venison burgers 20

Watermelon crush 76